This gallery of portraits is dedicated

TO ALL MEN
OF LETTERS
& PEOPLE OF
SUBSTANCE

by **ROBERTO DE VICQ DE CUMPTICH**

DAVID R. GODINE, PUBLISHER

To Tia Maria Helena,
who showed me the lay of the land and
to Tia Vanje who showed me
what lies beyond
that . . .

When we speak of painting as a portrait in words, we are, of course, speaking metaphorically. We mean that a writer uses letters and phrases to create an image in the imagination, and then, through that miraculous neurological process known as reading, the reader translates the verbal into the pictorial and presto! a visual image appears in the reader's mind.

How unusual, how clever, and above all how thrilling of Roberto de Vicq de Cumptich to have shortcircuited that relatively lengthy process and made the metaphorical literal: to have created these marvelous portraits using actual words and flourishes of decorative lettering. It reminds us of what every writer and designer knows – how much can be accomplished with language. These witty drawings show us how much nuance, personality, and emotion can be expressed by combining letters to trace the features of the human face.

In these revealing renderings, the various fonts seem to have been invented especially to convey the character of each particular writer. What, besides these curlicues of Ex Ponto, could have so elegantly given us the waves of Racine's wig? The arabesques of Avalon describe perfectly the sophistication (and the less often recognized tenderness) of Oscar Wilde, just as Nuevo seems to have been designed to convey something quintessentially aristocratic and Russian about Vladimir Nabokov. The second half of the book performs the ultimate magic trick: using the abstraction of the emblematic graphic image to give a particular face to a broad, abstract concept.

In one of his stories, Paul Bowles writes about the music of marks on paper: "The tiny inkmarks of which a symphony consists may have been made long ago, but when they are fulfilled in sound they become imminent and mighty." So, in these ingenious portraits, Roberto de Vicq de Cumptich has managed to make the alphabet sing.

MEN
LETT

In 2000 I did an alphabet book for my daughter, called *Bembo's Zoo*. The whole book was illustrated with animal images using only the letters of their names. When it was time to publish the book, my editor asked me for an author's photo for the book flap. Most people over thirty hate to see themselves in pictures. So I decided, then, to use the same process, to make my own portrait. From then on I started creating portraits of writers.

I tried to match the typefaces in two ways, the first to the style of the writing and the second to a peculiar feature of their faces. An example of the first is the late Kurt Vonegut with the typeface Aja, a typeface that is both fanciful and captures the style of his time (the sixties). The mane of Oscar Wilde or Mark Twain's moustache have their equivalent shapes respectively in the characters D of Avalon and W in Cochin.

A letter is much more than a representation of a symbol, a letter depicts a time period, a certain mood and perhaps, in this book, the soul of the artist.

O F
E R S

PUBLISHER'S NOTE: *You may wonder (as we did at first) what the numbers adjoining the names on the grids mean. Here's the dope: the portraits are set from the letters of the font, which is identified. The numbers reveal how many times a given letter is used in the construction of the portrait. Sort of an alphabetical* Where's Waldo?

2

3 4 2 4

Maya *1928

Angelou

6 4 9 2 2 4

CLARENDON   ARTHUR

*1915 †2005   Miller

16 2 10 9   1 6

1 4 1 2 3 2

TRUMAN | Capote

*1924 | †1984 | MODERN

*1882 †1941   123 5 2 2

JAMES Joyce

BASKERVILLE

GOLDEN
COCKEREL

3 4 8   2 4 44 3 5 |*1915

Saul Bellow |†2005

SALMAN Rushdie

*1947   2 2 4 3 2 3 2

Emily Dickinson   *Delphin*

3 2 1 13 6 2 1 1 4   2 1   *1830   †1886

Evelyn Waugh

10

*1854 †1900

OSCAR *Avalon*

Wilde

1 4 127 3

+1835 Cochin **M A R K**

+1910 *Twain*

3 14 5 2 3

STEPHEN *King*

3 2 4 3

*1947

Grimshaw Hand

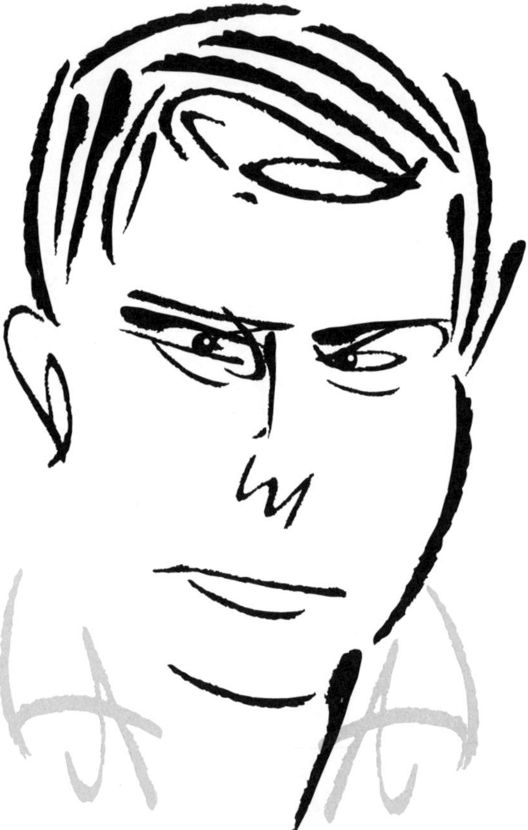

WILLIAM *Shakespeare*

14

Elie Weisel *1928 †2007

1 6 4 1   3 1 3 3 1 7   Caflisch

EDGAR ALLAN POE

Oliver **WENDELL** *Holmes* Linoscript

1 2 3 3 2 1   1 1 2 3

∗1841

†1935

George Orwell

18 *1819 †1891

Herman Melville

7
1
1
2
1
2
1
3

2
2
3
2
1
2

*1891 †1980

7
2
4
4
10
1

12
7
5
1
3

Mezz

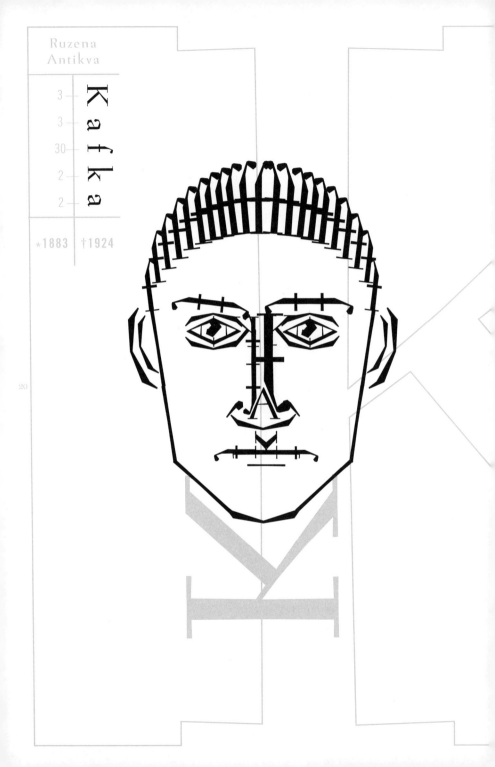

Kurt Vonnegut

22

Joseph
Conrad

*1857 †1924

2 1 5 1 2 1

3 1 1 1 1 8

Voluta Script

J.M.

Coetzee

*1940

24

Bookman

*1911 | †1983

5 1 4 4   1 1

Tennessee

Williams

4 5 2 3 5 7   5 1

Tom Wolfe

26

Ayn Rand

*1882 †1941 *Didot*

Virginia Woolf

3 1 2 1 1 2 1 1   2 1 1 2 1

1 2 1 2 1 1 1 12 | *1899

Vladimir

Nabokov

† 1977

Nueva

3 1 2 1 1 1

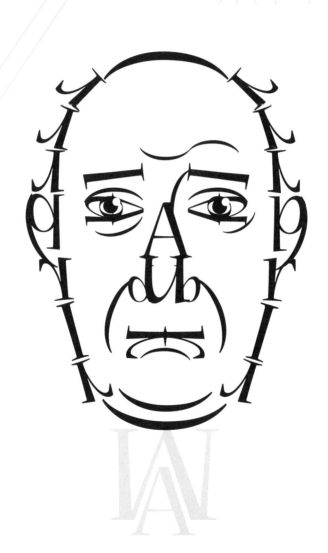

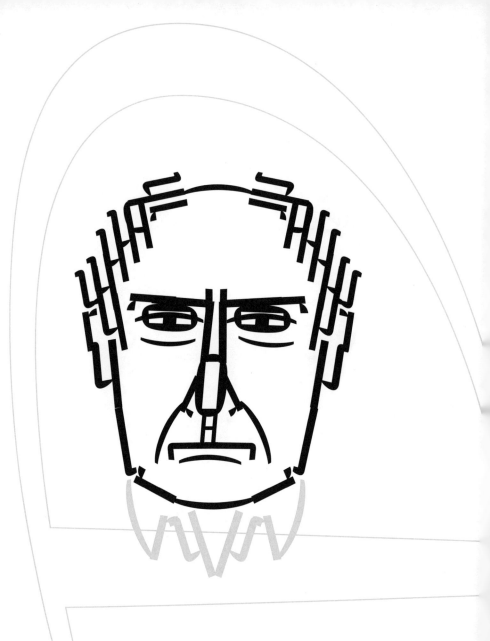

Calcite

Philip Roth

*1933

1 9 1 4 1 1   12 3 2 8

Trade Gothic

*1933

†2004

Susan Sontag

3 1 2 1 1 2 1 1 2 1 1

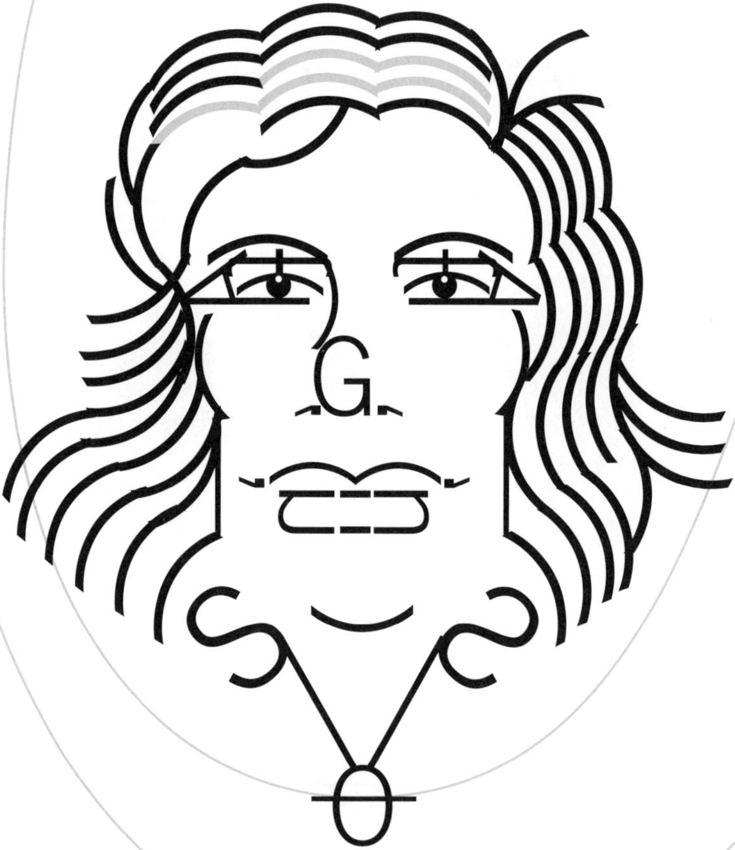

Samuel Beckett

*1906
†1989

William Faulkner | †1962

34

William

Burroughs

Francine Prose

Wittenberger
Fraktur

12 4 4 2 10 8 2 4   4 3 2 3 4

*1947

MARCEL

*1871

†1922

proust

AURIOL

George Bernard Shaw

1 1 1 2 1 1 2 3 1 2 2 4 3 1

John Steinbeck

Bodoni
Old Face

1902 | 1968

CRONOS | John Updike

*1932   1   4 2   1 2 2 19 1 1

Mrs. Eaves

John Irving

^1942   23   4 1 1 4 5   2

Capital Script

2 1 3 1 3 1 2   8 7 3 4 1 4 2 1

Gustave Flaubert

*1821

†1880

Graham

Greene

2P SUBS

There is a part of the human brain whose sole purpose is to identify facial patterns. A product of our evolution, this bit of specialization aided and protected our ancestors, who, in order to survive, learned to recognize faces: eyes darker than foreheads, cheeks bigger and lighter than mouths. From generalized smiley faces to e-mail emoticons to the man in the moon, we are constantly looking to reconstruct this pattern and to recognize it.

AUTUMN

46

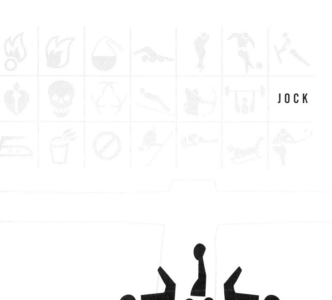

JOCK

MOTHER
NATURE

FATHER
TIME

PHILANDERER

SOCIAL
BUTTERFLY

OH!

PINKO

PASSIVE

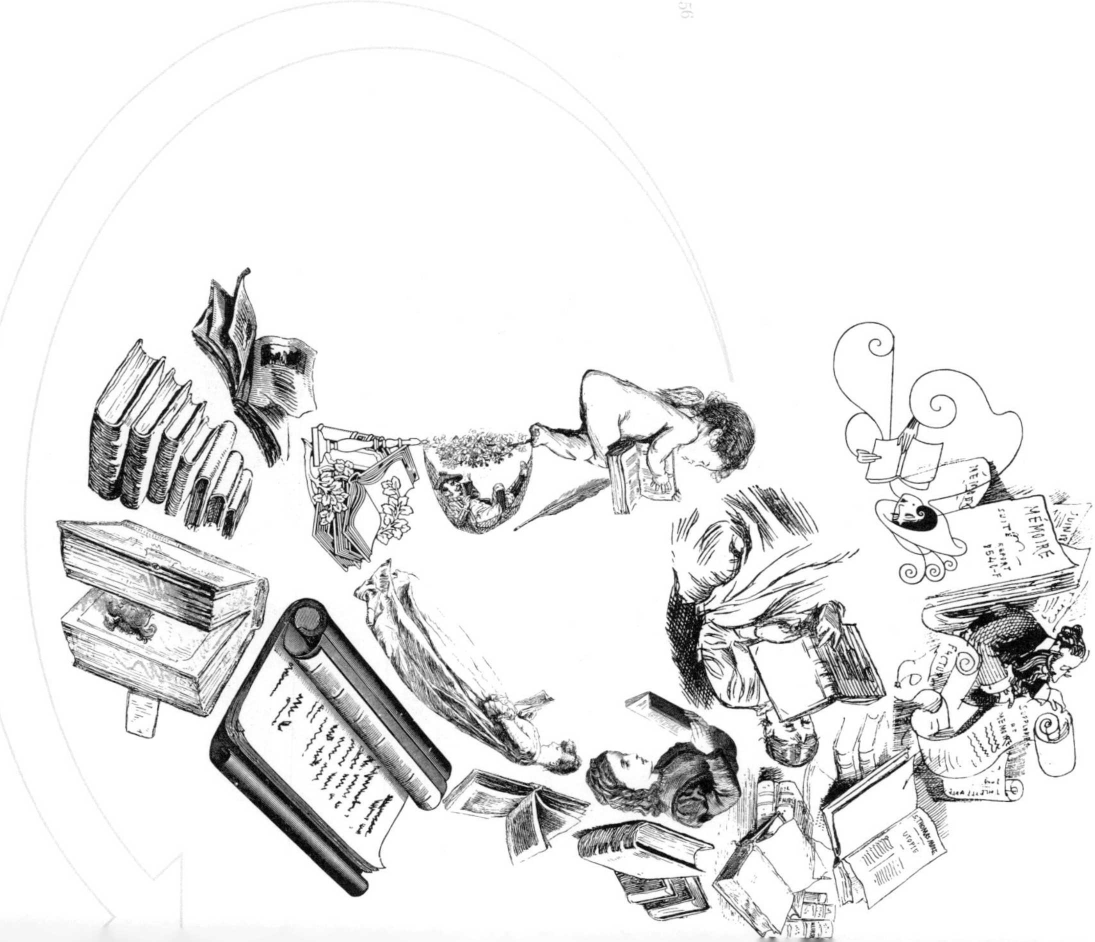

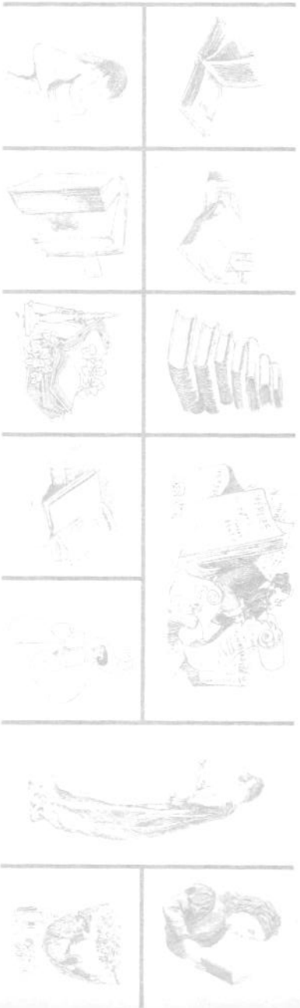

ACTIVE

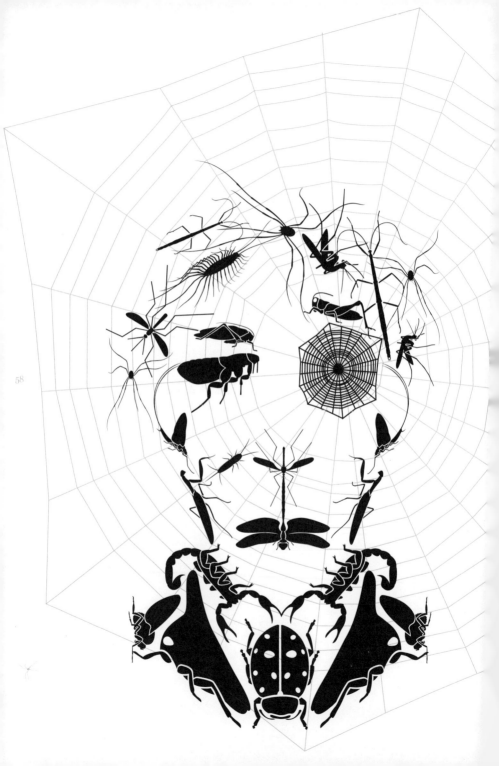

GRATITUDE

THANKSGIVING

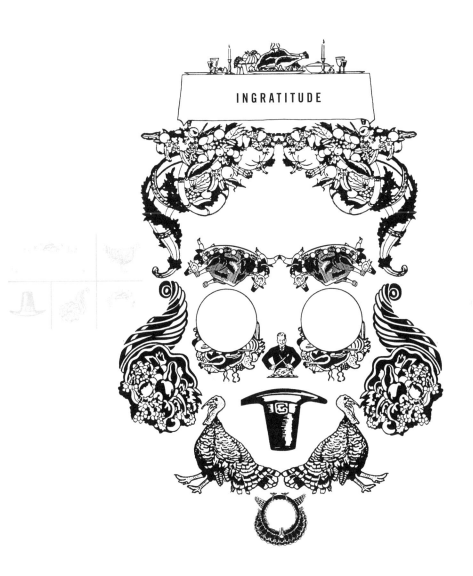

62

NAUGHTY

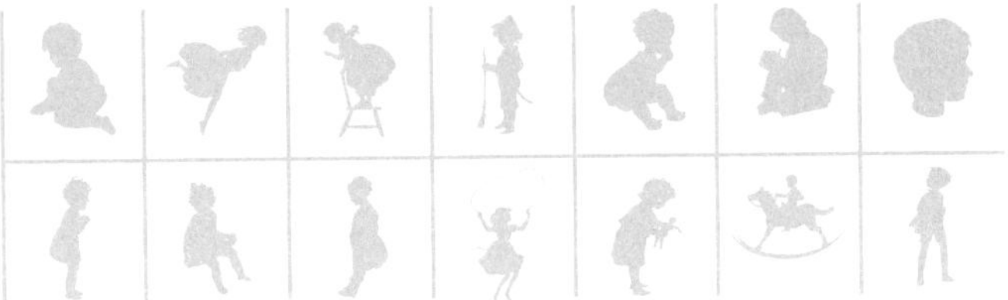

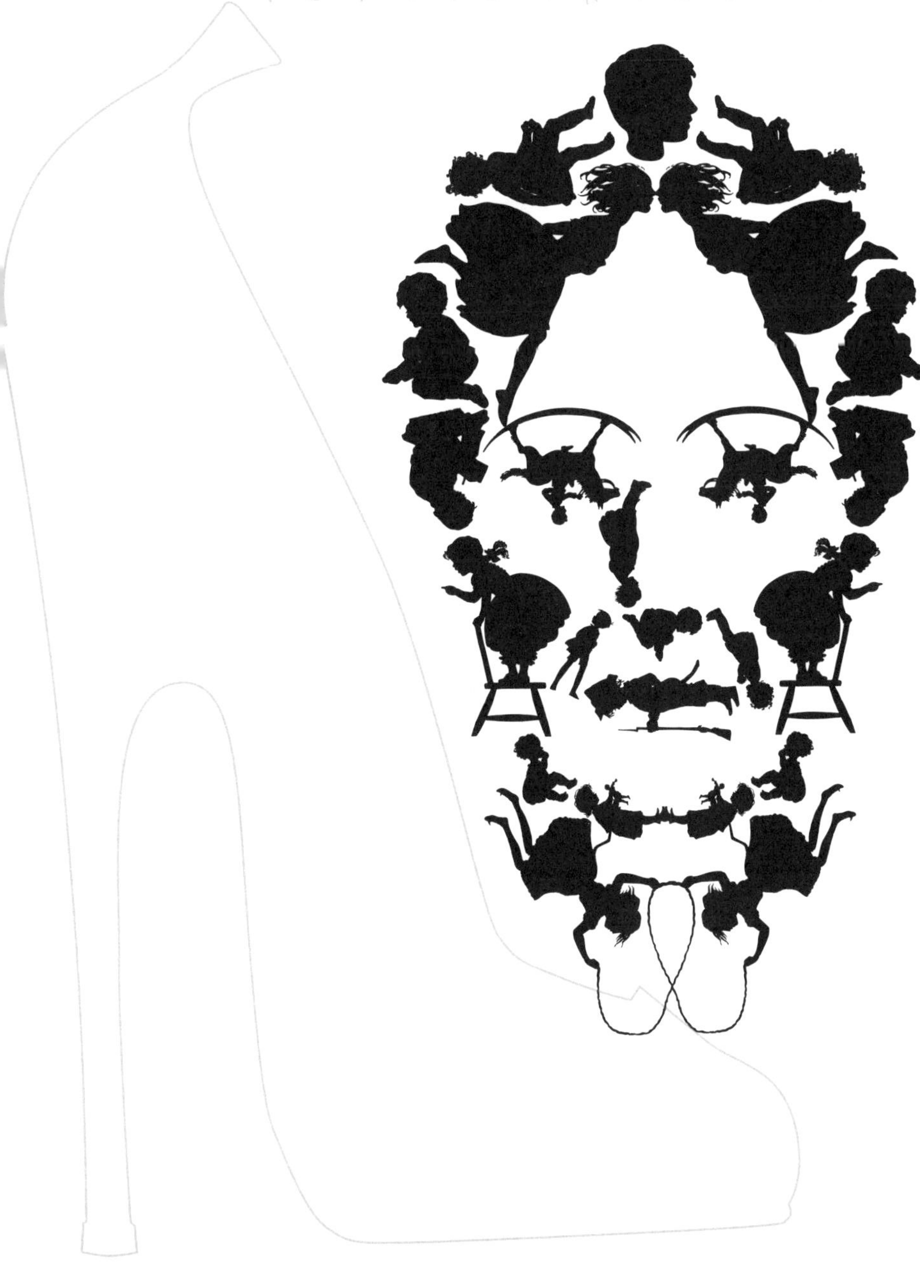

G O

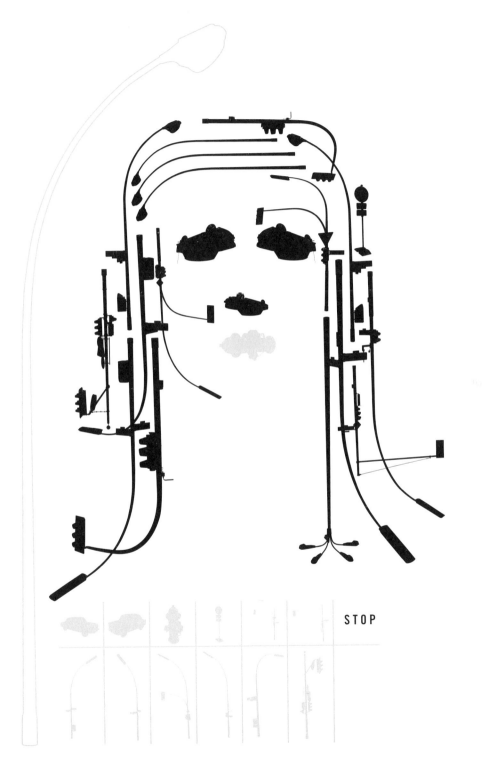

STOP

66

COOKED

RAW

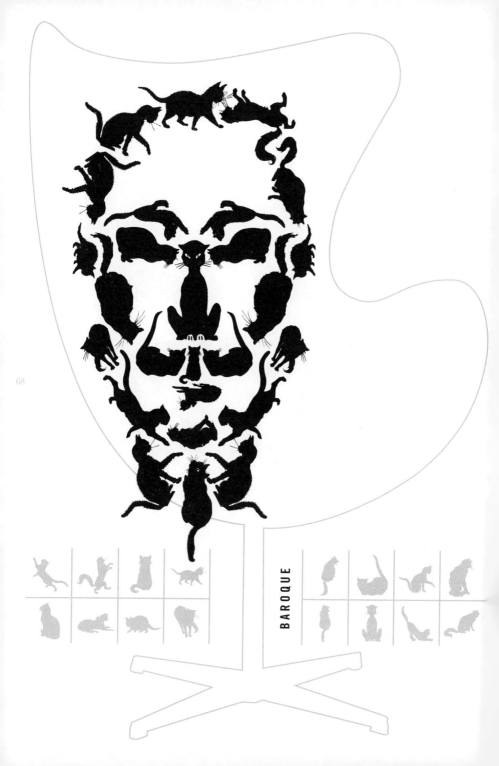

BAROQUE

MODERN

70

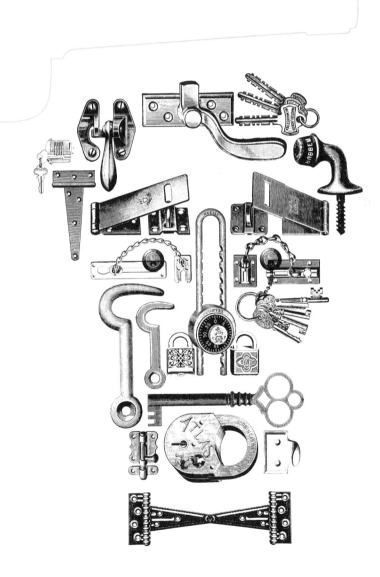

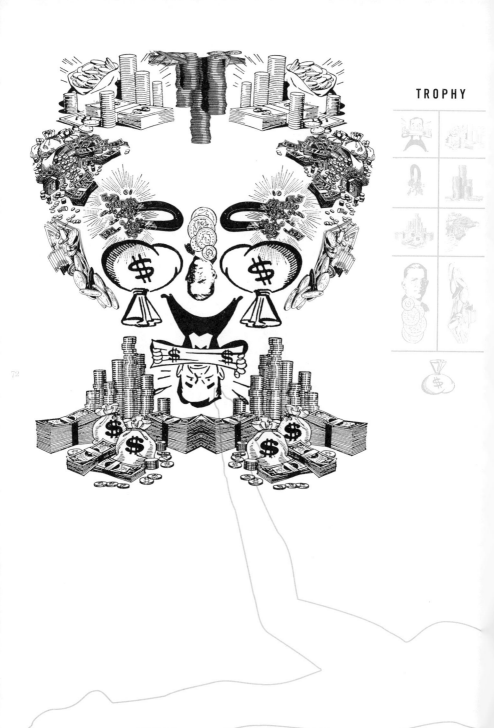

TROPHY

WIFE

LOVE

BIRD

LAUNDRY

OPINION

BEAUTY

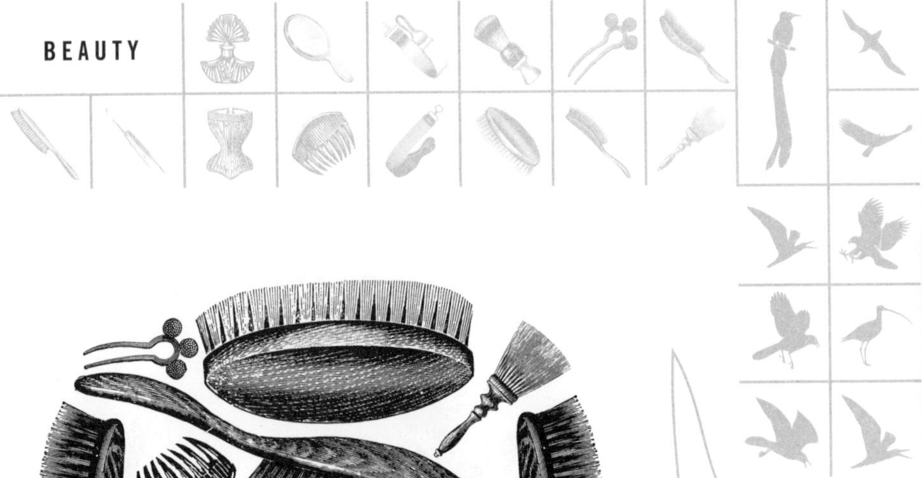

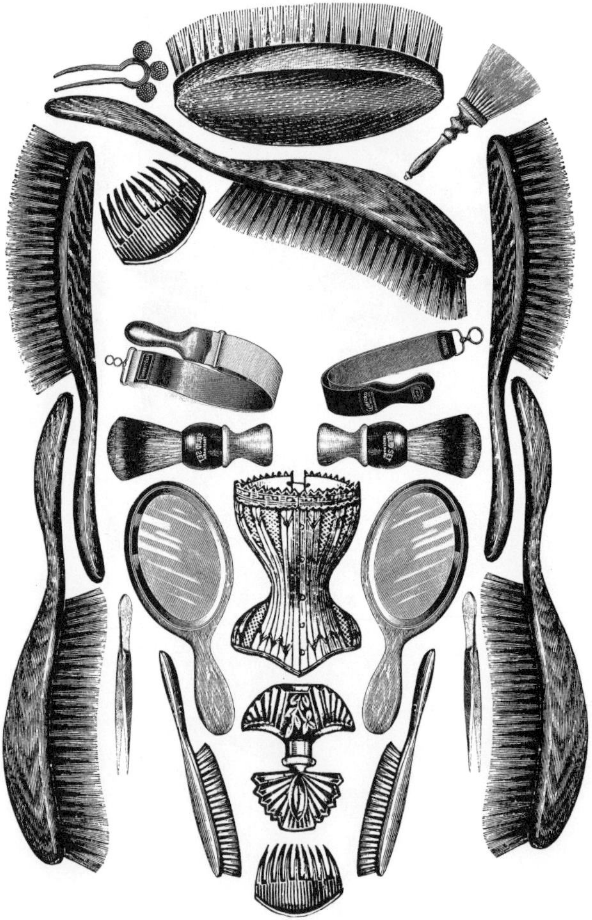

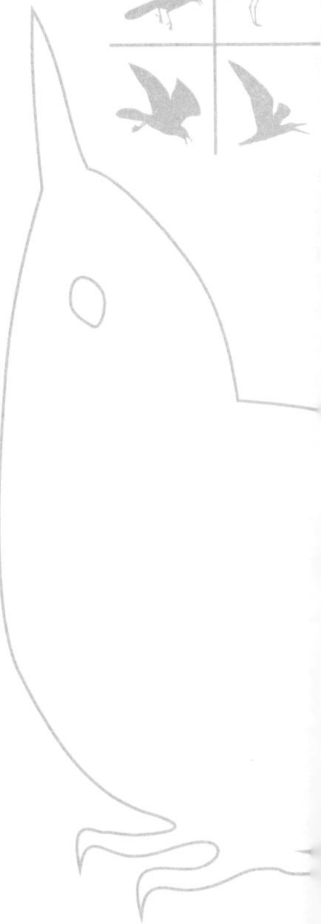

84

TURF

86

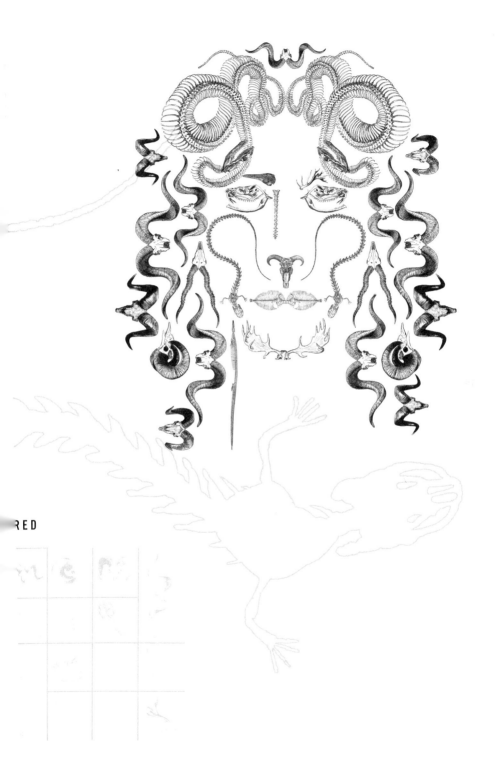